Beautiful

Vermont

"Learn about America in a beautiful way."

Beautiful
Vermont

Concept and Design: Robert D. Shangle
Text: James Michael Fagan

First Printing October, 1980
Published by Beautiful America Publishing Company
P.O. Box 608, Beaverton, Oregon 97075
Robert D. Shangle, Publisher

Library of Congress Cataloging in Publication Data
Beautiful Vermont
1. Vermont—Description ahd travel—1951—Views. I. Title.
F50.F4   917.43   80-14775
ISBN 0-89802-105-7
ISBN 0-89802-104-9 (Paperback)

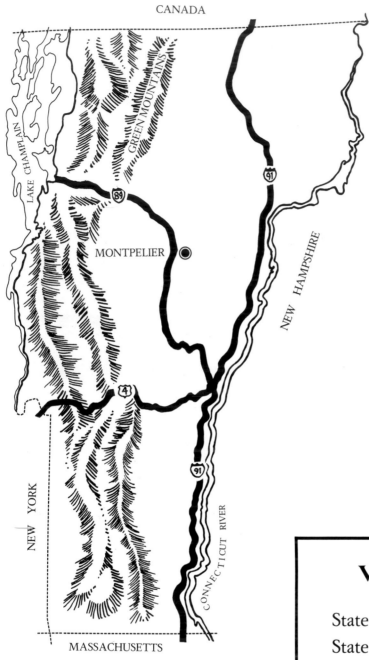

CANADA

LAKE CHAMPLAIN

GREEN MOUNTAINS

89

MONTPELIER

91

NEW HAMPSHIRE

4

91

CONNECTICUT RIVER

NEW YORK

MASSACHUSETTS

N

VERMONT

State Capital: *Montpelier*

State Flower: *Red Clover*

State Bird: *Thrush*

State Motto: *Vermont, Freedom, and Unity*

State Nickname: *Green Mountain State*

Contents

Enlarged Prints

Most of the photography in this book is available as photographic
enlargements. Send self-addressed, stamped envelope for information.
For a complete product catalog, send $1.00.
Beautiful America Publishing Company
P.O. Box 608
Beaverton, Oregon 97075

Photo Credits

GENE AHRENS—*page 20; page 21; page 30; page 34; page 64.*

JAMES BLANK—*page 17; page 27; page 49; page 53; page 54; page 58; page 61.*

BOB CLEMENZ—*page 19; pages 24-25; page 38; pages 40-41; page 44; page 46; page 48; pages 56-57.*

GRANT HAIST—*page 35; page 37; page 59.*

HAMPFLER STUDIO—*page 23.*

JOHN HILL—*page 18; page 22; page 26; page 31; page 33; page 36; page 39; page 43; page 45; page 47; page 50; page 51; page 52; page 60; page 62.*

JOHN HOPKINS—*page 29; page 42.*

HUGH MCKENNA—*page 55.*

PHILIP MILLER—*page 28; page 63.*

DON STEUCK—*page 32.*

Color Separations
by
Universal Color Corporation
Beaverton, Oregon/San Diego, California

Introduction

Two resources stand out over all the rest that Vermont has been blessed with since her beginning. Those are, simply said, her land, and her people. You cannot overstate the terrific beauty of this land. And, too, it is quite impossible to know the people of Vermont without admiring them profoundly. While Vermonters protectively watch over their land with an iron-like tenacity, their Roman goddess, Ceres, watches over them. To know this land, you must know her people. Likewise, to know Vermonters, you must know their land. There is a certain richness in the people that will always remain nondescript.

The earliest settlers—the Indians, French, English, and Yankees—of this region we now call Vermont were all independent thinkers, who fought for their freedom and their homes, and who learned to survive through extraordinary hardships. Because Vermont is a land that only rewards persistent industry, the pioneers who settled this area developed the skills in discipline needed to conquer this frontier.

The legend of Ethan Allen and his Green Mountain Boys probably most accurately characterizes the people of Vermont and their stormy struggle to gain sovereignty for their state.

Verd, meaning green in French, and *mont*, meaning mountain, Vermont derives its identity from its enchantingly beautiful green mountains. Vermont's unsurpassed scenery is a pearl in the country's cache of most beloved treasures. There is never a more memorable moment than when you gaze upon hillside after hillside, all aglow with the truly spectacular red, orange, and yellow hues of the Vermont maples. Maple trees, all ablaze in autumn, are set off by a rich tapestry of evergreens. It is this gorgeous land that Vermonters have conquered, defended, and learned to love.

This fascinating state and its people will introduce you to Lake Champlain, and its lovely port city, Burlington. Stowe, the ski capital of the East, is one of several winter resorts equipped with exquisite facilities. The world's largest marble and granite quarries, located in Proctor and Barre, are truly a fascinating phenomenon and education for the whole family.

Bernard De Voto, a famous writer, expressed his feelings about the Green Mountain State this way: ''There is no more Yankee than Polynesian in me, but whenever I go to Vermont, I feel I am traveling toward my home place.''

Green Mountains

Perhaps it is the Green Mountains that are most responsible for imprinting those well-known traits of today's and yesterday's Vermonters—independent thinking, and a frontiersman's stick-to-itiveness attitude.

Long, rigorous winters and short growing seasons demanded hard labor from the early settlers. The old discipline of the frontier molded Vermont men and women into an industrious and proud people. It was the rugged personality of the Green Mountains that seemed to imprint a noble character on its people: stubborn and independent, with a marked self-reliance.

Vermont, named after its greatest gift, the Green Mountains, is blessed with the rugged beauty of the mountain range that strikes out through the center of the state. Dotted with hundreds of snow-capped mountain peaks during the winter, and frosted with countless acres of majestic evergreen trees year round, this northern link of the Appalachian system serves up a winter playground treat that is visited by thousands every year.

Most attractive to tourists and natives alike is the region's excellent ski facilities. Stowe, a small mountain village located north of the heart of the Green Mountains, is easily accessible via State Highway 100. This ski resort/summer vacationland owes much of its fame to the location of Vermont's highest peak, Mt. Mansfield. Renowned as the ski capital of the East, Stowe is bestowed with more than 50 resorts accommodating 3,000 skiers. The longtime slogan, ''there's always snow in Stowe'' is a dream come true for winter athletes. The average ski season lasts from mid-December through late April. Mt. Mansfield provides enough space for many acres of open slopes and several miles of ski trails. A four-passenger gondola lifts skiers and tourists up the tall slopes.

Within sight of Mt. Mansfield is historic Smugglers' Notch. As the story goes, Congress declared an embargo in the early 1800s that made it illegal to buy from or sell goods to Britain, or its colonies. Vermont's border-line location with Canada made it a favorite route for smugglers. Such a large volume of illegal goods and cattle flowed both ways through the pass near Cambridge, beside Mt. Mansfield, that the place became known as Smugglers' Notch.

Gun fights between smugglers and border guards are long gone, but the tales are still passed on and continue to tickle every youngster's imagination.

The smugglers' hideout is now occupied by a lush and exciting vacation resort, The Village at Smugglers' Notch. Golf, swimming, night life, riding stables, tennis, fishing—recreation and relaxation are the only concerns at the present day Smugglers' Notch.

The ski tow, incidentally, first came into being in 1933 when two Woodstock, Vermont men saw an opportunity for downhill skiing at the nearby Suicide Six ski area. The winter resort is appropriately named for its 500-foot vertical drop located on the slopes.

Other popular and well-equipped ski areas include Glen Ellen, Killington, Mad River, Stratton, and Sugarbush. Their summits are all at, or around, the 4,000-foot level. The Sugarbush Valley ski area, located near Warren, has one of the longest ski lifts in the East, an aerial gondola. The region around Roxbury, a quiet country village just east of Warren, is particularly renowned for its brilliant autumn coloring.

The Taconic Mountains, trailing up along the New York-Vermont border in the state's southwest corner, are generally too low for skiing. But nestled in among the Taconics is the largest natural body of water lying entirely within the state, Lake Bomoseen of Castleton. One of the most highly developed summer recreation areas in the Green Mountain State, Bomoseen occupies a rocky basin surrounded by low, forested hills and blunted mountains. It was in this beautiful, crystal-clear lake in 1830 where a local boy, Julio T. Buel, invented the fishing spoon, after accidentally dropping a table spoon into the water. Seeing big fish lunge at the spoon started the young inventor on his way to fishing stardom. In addition, picturesque Lake Bomoseen was a favorite summer spot for comedian Harpo Marx.

Starting at the southernmost border of Vermont, where the Hoosac Mountains of Massachusetts become the Green Mountains, any outdoorsman can head north and quickly find his paradise. Meandering through rolling country landscapes and majestically craggy mountains, the vacationing traveler will discover why so many residents call their Vermont home ''the closest thing to heaven.''

Fertile valleys and more than 400 lakes and ponds cut through Vermont and the Green Mountains, forming an area of scenic variety unequaled in New England. Nearing some towns, the alert visitor can sometimes sight a tall steeple before crossing the last verdant meadow into one of Vermont's many historic towns.

Brilliant autumn colors are how many remember this lovely state. The flaming reds and yellows of maple trees are sprinkled everywhere in the rugged mountains and rolling meadows. Since the days when the Indians first showed the early settlers that there was "sweet food in trees," nothing has been so typical of Vermont as the first cry of the season, "Saps a runnin'!" From the earliest times to the present, one of the greatest joys of childhood has been "sugar-on-the-snow"—that wonderful experience of pouring a dipper of pure boiling syrup on gleaming white snow. Nature's gift solidifies immediately into sweet candy. A little-known fact about these maples is that the sugar in their sap is responsible for turning the leaves to their brilliant colors.

Added to Nature's beautiful landscapes and sparkling maple trees, one first discovers Vermont's most treasured manmade landmark, the covered bridge. Every one of Vermont's 114 covered bridges has a story behind it, and each one illustrates a feeling of lasting romance among the people of Vermont for these treasured landmarks. Contrary to local legend, the bridges were not built to provide cover for courting couples during inclement weather. Vermonters are too practical and thrifty for such frivolity. The bridges were built to provide protection from the weather for the wooden-planked roadway. Out-of-state visitors should not hesitate to ask local Vermonters about the history of any covered bridge. A proud heritage surrounds these rare landmarks. The Green Mountain State has more covered bridges than all of the other New England states together.

For the enthusiastic hiker who wants to absorb all of these Vermont wonderments, and yet wants to get off the beaten path, the Long Trail is the perfect route. The Long Trail guides the hiker through the peaks of the main Green Mountain range, starting at the Massachusetts border and winding north to the Canadian frontier. It is a 261-mile trail beginning near Williamstown of Massachusetts. There are about 170 miles of side and approach trails. The entire system includes approximately 425 miles. The Green Mountain Club, formed in 1910 by 23 hikers, maintains most of the trail system. The club members in 1910, led by James P. Taylor, then principal of Vermont Academy at Saxtons River, gave of their time and money to forge this "Footpath in the Wilderness." The club finished the trail 18 years later, in 1928.

The Trail is more often taken from south to north. By traveling in this direction, hikers enjoy an unbroken scenic extravaganza, conquering the vistas of New York's Adirondacks, Lake Champlain, and the White Mountains that rise in the north. Continuing the hike through the rolling, timbered hills at the southern end and on through the distinctive Taconics to the west completes the trip.

For the outdoors enthusiast who prefers water travel, they should know that because of the Green Mountains' central mass, Vermont rivers either flow east in the

Connecticut River on the Vermont-New Hampshire border, or west into Lake Champlain. The Missiquoi, Lamoille, and Winooski rivers are three interesting exceptions to this rule. All three rise in the east, and flow directly through the Green Mountains emptying into Lake Champlain. According to state geologists, these three exceptions ran in their present courses before the Green Mountains were formed, 350 million years ago. At that time, it is reported that Vermont's main mountain range was probably as high as the Alps.

It is a just tribute to the Green Mountain State that a number of writers and poets found a comfortable and private haven here for their work. San Francisco native Robert Frost settled in Ripton near Middlebury College's Bread Loaf School of English. The poet's dry, piercing wit and solid good sense made him popular with his Vermont neighbors. Frost's Ripton cabin, located in the east-central part of the state, is open to the public by advance appointment.

Whether it is solitude you are longing for, or an outdoor adventure custom made for daring the sportsman, the Green Mountains will oblige your company.

Valley of Vermont

The Valley of Vermont, nestled in between the Taconic Mountains on the west and the Green Mountains on the east, is the site of some of the state's wealthiest resources. Several fun-filled and fascinating afternoons await the visitor who needs only to meander along U.S. Highway 7 and its side roads. The highway runs north and south along the valley's floor.

One of America's finest trout streams, the Batten Kill, is minutes away from Highway 7. Also conveniently situated on the highway are the great marble treasures of Danby and East Dorset. The marble quarried from these sites was used to construct some of the nation's most magnificent monuments, including the stunning Supreme Court Building in Washington, D.C. Rutland County is known to Vermonters as the third best hunting area in the state. And the city of Bennington is alive with history about the famous Green Mountain Boys, and their colorful leader, Ethan Allen.

This long and beautiful valley, which begins at the Massachusetts-Vermont border and continues as far north as Brandon, is sprinkled with treasures awaiting an appreciative discoverer.

Starting in the south and traveling north where the valley widens into the Champlain Valley, the visitor will first discover charming and historic Bennington. Here is where the famous (or infamous) Green Mountain Boys and Ethan Allen planned their war strategies. The small army of men was instrumental in establishing Vermont as the 14th state and helping to protect the country's northern border from the British invaders in the American Revolution, and in the War of 1812.

In the first few years of the 1770 decade, it was Ethan Allen and his Green Mountain Boys who carved out a very unique niche in the history of the United States. The ''Green Mountain Boys against the world'' is a legend that describes what seemed to be a civil war between neighboring British provinces, New York and New Hampshire.

Caused by an unsettled boundary dispute between the New York and New Hampshire provinces, settlers' land claims to the Vermont area differed, depending upon which province issued the title. Governors Benning Wentworth of New

Hampshire and George Clinton of New York both granted land titles in the disputed territory. When landowners came together, there were long and bitter struggles.

In 1770, during this time of ''bogus land claims,'' the Green Mountain Boys were organized under Allen's colorful leadership. Declared heroes by the New Hampshire settlers, and called the ''Bennington Mob'' by New Yorkers, Allen's well-organized army relentlessly drove 'Yorkers away from their Vermont home.

Their meeting place was the Green Mountain Tavern, kept by Stephen Fay in Bennington. Over the tavern sign hung a stuffed catamount (mountain lion) with bared teeth, snarling defiance toward the New York border. Today, an historic monument marks the site of the Old Catamount Tavern in Bennington.

In what proved to be a final test of will between New Yorkers and the Green Mountain Boys, New York sent a force of 300 men under Sheriff Ten Eyck to seize the Breakenridge farm of Bennington from the ''outlaw mobsters.'' Seth Warner, captain of the Bennington Company of the Green Mountain Boys, owned the farm. News of the New York force spread and the men of Bennington quickly took up muskets, pistols, clubs, scythes, and pitchforks, and drove back Ten Eyck and his posse at the covered bridge, located near the threatened farm. That same sturdy bridge still stands today, just beyond the site of Warner's house in Bennington.

Ethan Allen came to be known as the ''Robin Hood of Vermont.'' He and a few of his Green Mountain Boys had prices put on their heads by the state of New York. By some historians, Allen and his group were considered heroes. Others labeled them outlaws. Whatever the personal opinion, Ethan Allen was instrumental in establishing Vermont as an independent state.

In Old Bennington a stately 306-foot monument commemorates the Battle of Bennington, which some historians call the turning point of the American Revolution. It was near here that Colonel John Stark, aided by Colonel Seth Warner and 350 of his Green Mountain Boys, successfully fought back the British and their German reinforcements. This loss slowed the British greatly and was later credited for turning the tide of victory toward the Americans. Today an elevator whisks you to the top of the monument to look out on the peaceful panorama that was once engulfed in fierce battle. A beautiful diorama, painted inside the monument, tells the story of the battle.

History abounds in Bennington. Hanging in the truly fascinating Bennington Museum is the oldest Stars and Stripes in existence, the famous Bennington flag. There are also extensive displays of military memorabilia, colonial furniture, American glass, Bennington pottery, and a large collection of Grandma Moses' delightful paintings.

The valley's most important river, and also the longest in the state, is Otter

Creek. The sportsman, who prefers paddle travel to Highway 7, will find this river easily navigable for his canoe. There are several beautiful campgrounds along this river, which is locally called the Big Otter. Rising in Mt. Tabor Town, the long waterway flows 75 miles northward, emptying into Lake Champlain. Dozens of covered bridges cross the creek. Ending at Vergennes, the Big Otter also offers excellent fishing as it winds through some of the more spectacular sections of the Taconic and Green Mountains.

Local fishermen, willing to share their favorite holes, might tell you about those elusive trout in the famous Batten Kill, located near West Arlington. One of America's finest trout streams, the Batten Kill, and neighboring Waloomsac River, occupies the western section of the Valley of Vermont.

Rupert, located west of Highway 7 near the New York border, has the distinction of having had Vermont's only short-lived mint. In 1785, when Vermont was an independent republic, Reuben Harman was granted the exclusive right to mint coins. For three years he minted copper pennies. Those distinctive coins are now prized by collectors.

Due east on Highway 7 is East Dorset. A gleam of excitement uplifted this slumbering town in 1785, when the first marble deposits in the United States were discovered here. The Mt. Aeolus quarries started a minor "marble rush" in the state. No longer worked today, the high-quality marble quarried at this site went into the building of the New York Public Library.

Today the busy quarries at Danby and Proctor are responsible for Vermont leading the nation in the production of marble. The magnificent Supreme Court Building, the Lincoln Memorial, and portions of the nation's Capitol building were built with Danby marble. The headquarters of the Vermont Marble Company in Proctor has been called the "center of the marble world." Most of the public buildings and even the sidewalks are made of the gleaming white stone. It's a genuine thrill to walk these streets lined with marble. The well-kept village appears glacial white against the emerald green fields of Otter Creek Valley.

The state also ranks as the country's leading producer of granite, and mines about 90 percent of the nation's asbestos. Barre, further north and east, is known as the world's granite center. The Vermont Asbestos Company operations are based in Lowell, located in north-central Vermont.

While traveling along U.S. Highway 7 in this area, the weary motorist can take a refreshing break at one of two popular summer resorts. Clarendon Springs and Manchester, both located on, or near the highway, are ranked high on visitors' lists of things to do and places to see.

For the visitor with winter recreation in mind, the Alpine Slide is only minutes away at Bromley Mountain. A chairlift glides you to the 3,260-foot summit lookout for a breathtaking glimpse of the five surrounding states. The more adventurous souls can disembark earlier, board a sled, and ''swoosh'' down nearly a mile of hairpin turns, curves, and straightaways. It is an invigorating slide that is safe and exciting.

The museum that says it all on marble—the world famous marble exhibit at the Vermont Marble Company in Proctor—is an interesting and enjoyable stop for children and adults alike. Impressive displays of marble from all over the world, and the chance to watch a sculptor at work, makes this visit a memorable one. Marble gifts and table tops are available here at low factory prices.

The Valley of Vermont offers a wide variety of fun things to do, and fascinating places to see. Visitors who spend time here often feel the warm hospitality of the residents and their gracious homes. It's a particular way of life. No one characteristic completely describes the good feeling one senses when experiencing the Valley.

Champlain Valley

The gentle, rolling hills and meadows of beautiful Champlain Valley have enticed every man since Samuel de Champlain, and the Algonquian and Iroquois Indians first called this place their own.

The quiet beauty of Champlain Valley sharply betrays its stormy history. Where ferocious Indian battles and testy conflicts between the French, English, and Yankees once engulfed the area, a relaxed pace and sweet feeling of secure quiet now rules the valley.

Some say the Champlain Valley was designed as a paradise away from home for the original Creator of the land. ''Enchanting'' is what others call it. All agree that they feel a restful ease when experiencing this wonderful gift of nature.

The graceful Vermont Lowlands-Lake Champlain area is situated between the Green Mountains on the east, and New York's Adirondack Mountains on the west. The valley opens out toward Canada from its southern point at Brandon. (One out of every five Vermonters lives in this region.)

Champlain Valley residents often frequent the state's largest and most beautiful city, Burlington. In addition they religiously take time to enjoy their other rich resources in smaller St. Albans, in the college town of Middlebury, in historical Vergennes, and in the many other rural towns.

Champlain Valley is steeped in a history of several peoples warring over its riches. Indians traveling through this region capitalized on the excellent hunting and fishing grounds. Bristol Pond, just north of Bristol, was used as a rendezvous point, where Indians chipped their arrowheads and spearheads from local rock. Today the muddy-bottomed pond offers excellent fishing, and is especially well stocked with pickerel. For the Indians the region served as an important transportation route between north and south. The Algonquian tribes struggled for several years to protect this territory from the fierce warriors of the Iroquois of the southwest.

The French were the first western colonists to discover these North American lowlands. It was at Chimney Point on July 4, 1609 that French leader and explorer

Village on the Waits River

State Capitol Building, Montpelier

North end of Grand Island

19

South Woodbury

Willoughby Lake

21

Covered bridge near Pittsfield

Autumn scene
(Following pages) Keiser Pond near Peacham

Ferry dock on the west side of Grand Island

The Connecticut River south of St. Johnsbury

Covered footbridge at West Danville

Autumn scene

29

Craftsbury Common

Big Falls south of North Troy

31

East Dorset

Sunset on Lake Champlain

Central Vermont
(Following page) Stream near Mt. Mansfield

Mt. Mansfield from Pleasant Valley

35

East Topsham
(Preceding page) Church in Roxbury

Big Falls, south of Troy
(Following pages) East Corinth in autumn

Stream near North Bennington

East Topsham
(Preceding page) Old Constitution House, Windsor
(Second preceding page) Village Green and church at Lunenburg

Jenne Farm, Reading

Ethan Allen Monument, Burlington

Covered bridge near Harvey

Tunbridge

Stream near Stowe

East Orange

Birthplace of President Chester Arthur, near Fairfield

53

Farm in central Vermont

Old First Church, Bennington
(Following pages) Fall color near Peacham

Covered bridge over the Connecticut River, Windsor

Church in Roxbury

Sunset on Lake Champlain

60

Keeler Bay on Grand Island

Quinn Farm, West Woodstock

Samuel de Champlain first gazed upon a great body of water, and proudly named it after himself, Lake Champlain.

It was in this Lake Champlain region that the French explorer and his Algonquian Indian allies fought the first of many battles with the Iroquois. This was the first time the proud Iroquois had faced enemies who used the "white man's lightning." The Iroquois were soundly defeated, striking a severe blow to these warriors who considered themselves masters of the continent.

Ironically, it was this victory that eventually spelled disaster for the French colonists' hopes for the area. The Iroquois never forgave the French, and they never missed an opportunity to wage war with the invaders. One hundred and fifty years after the Champlain battle, angry Indians joined with their English allies to drive the French from the continent.

Although Champlain's discovery gave the French claim to the area, it was not until more than 50 years later that they attempted their first settlement. In 1666, 300 French soldiers, under Captain de La Motte, built a fortress with the timbers of the surrounding wilderness on an island in Lake Champlain. Today that northern island is named after the captain, Isle La Motte. The scene must have appeared strange to Indian onlookers. Here were French aristocrats, with their clean white shirt sleeves rolled back, directing the building in this remote wilderness, while the solemn, dark-robed Jesuit priests busied themselves with their clerical duties. The first Catholic mass in Vermont was celebrated at the completed Fort Saint Anne. The fort was established to defend French interests against the aggravated Mohawk Iroquois tribe. It was partly motivated by the Jesuit's religious zeal. It was abandoned, though, in less than 30 years, when a second French outpost was built at what is now Chimney Point.

Today St. Anne's Shrine and Isle La Motte are two of the more popular stops for visitors. The serene island village rests peacefully among apple orchards and several wooded acres. The Shrine of St. Anne is located here. The small chapel and other island facilities accommodate church and family groups. The Shrine is also the site of the famous statue of Samuel de Champlain, sculptured at Canada's Expo in 1967.

For well into the 18th century, Vermont was a "no man's land," a passageway for French and Indian raiding parties to harass English settlements. English colonists lived in fear of scalping attacks by the Algonquian Indians and their French allies. A daring raid in 1759, by Major Robert Rogers on the St. Francis Indians' headquarters far to the north in Canada, finally secured peace for the English settlements. The French gave up their century-long battle to colonize North America when they signed the Treaty of Paris in 1763, officially ending the French and Indian War.

The 1770s brought more wartime challenges to the young colonies and to the people of Champlain Valley. The American Revolution was the biggest undertaking yet for the hardy frontiersmen. Vermont's most famous and colorful person in history, Ethan Allen, again led the fight for self-rule.

The Revolution was a new and clearly legitimate cause for Allen and his Green Mountain Boys. The "Robin Hood of Vermont," together with his small army and the infamous Benedict Arnold, greatly helped the American independence effort. In their favorite Green Mountain Tavern, Arnold, Allen, and his boys plotted the impossible: the overthrow of the "impregnable" Fort Ticonderoga on the New York side of Lake Champlain. With a total force of 83 men, Vermont's freedom fighters captured a British stronghold that once had defeated an army of 15,000.

In the years after the American Revolution, there was some question about whether the independent-thinking Vermonters would ever join the Union. For 14 years Vermont acted as an independent republic. The sovereign state operated its own postal service, coined its own money, and naturalized citizens of other states and countries. Finally, in 1791, Vermont was accepted by Congress as the 14th state. Today the coins minted by the independent republic of Vermont are highly valued by collectors.

Vermonters, by now secure members of the United States, were especially conscious of a possible invasion by the British in the War of 1812. The valiant members of the 14th state, well known for their stubborn grip on freedom, controlled Lake Champlain and protected the country from a northern invasion.

Another test of Vermonters' will came in 1816, when the state was struck by the most crippling winter in its history. Referred to as "1800 and froze to death," there was a killing frost in every month of the year, and snow fell well into July and August.

Vermonters, always concerned about the individual and his welfare, demonstrated this concern when the slavery issue pitted the North against the South, in the War Between the States. There had never been any Negro slaves in Vermont, and the people were bitterly opposed to the idea. The legislature passed resolutions nearly every year condemning slavery and sent copies of their opinion to each of the southern states. Georgia responded with a resolution asking the President to dig a ditch around Vermont so that "the thing could be sailed away on the ocean." During this time the state was instrumental in helping slaves escape to Canada on the underground railroad. The western towns of Fair Haven and St. Albans were major stations on the Vermont section of the railroad.

Vermont maintained its reputation for prompt readiness in conflict, when the legislature voted a million dollars for use in World War I. This is especially notable because the action was taken even before the United States entered the war.

Again, always ready, the Vermonters didn't wait for the mother country to enter the second world war. "In 1941, the good people of that state got so enraged at the Nazis that they declared war on Germany two months before America did," reported newspaper columnist Charles Rice.

Visitors can catch a glimpse of Vermont's rich and long history by stopping at the famous and extensive Shelburne Museum. Located just south of Burlington, the interested history buff can step back into 300 years of American history.

Champlain Valley, rich in tales of its glorious past, is even more wealthy with its present resources. Burlington, a beautiful city, hosts scenic ferry trips across Lake Champlain, the nation's third largest natural freshwater lake outside of the Great Lakes. Sailing, power boating, canoeing, fishing, and winter ice-yachting provide some of the endless recreational opportunities in this lakeside city. A summer Mozart Festival adds to the visitor's delight.

St. Albans, a short drive due north from Burlington, hosts a fun-loving Maple Sugar Festival every spring. Parades, lumberjack contests, old-time fiddling, square dancing, trips to area sugar houses, and a rolling-pin-throwing competition are sure to entertain children and adults alike.

Minutes east of St. Albans is the birthplace of President Chester A. Arthur, in East Fairfield. Taking office following the assassination of one-time Vermont school-teacher President James Garfield, Arthur was an early supporter of civil rights. Arthur, like his Vermont countrymen, was instrumental in freeing slaves.

Nature lovers will not want to miss the 5,000-acre wildlife refuge of West Swanton, a birdwatcher's haven. The West Swanton/Swanton region, located in the northernmost portion of Lake Champlain near Quebec, offers unparalleled natural beauty. Another exciting attraction occurs here each spring when hundreds of fishermen from all over the eastern states try their luck on the walleyed pike.

The Champlain Valley is a place in which wide-eyed visitors immerse themselves for weeks. A home away from home, the region's rich history and lively tales of yesteryear's adventures, and its endless variety of dreamlike natural resources, make Champlain Valley a pearl in Vermont's treasury of jewels.

Piedmont and Northeast Kingdom

Common to both Vermont's Piedmont region and to the Northeast Kingdom are many scattered, beautiful lakes. This is Vermont's lake country. Fed by several mountain rivers and streams, the Piedmont is a rich reservoir of petite ponds and lakes large enough to accommodate boats and their anglers.

The Piedmont, as the name implies, is the eastern foot of the Green Mountains. The region begins where the Saxtons River joins the Connecticut River, and continues northward, gradually widening toward the Canadian frontier. The Northeast Highlands are outlined by Essex County, which is bordered by New Hampshire and Quebec, Canada.

Herein these two easterly regions lies most of the outstanding lake and pond fishing in the state. Vermont's charming capital city, Montpelier, conducts its business in this half of the Green Mountain State. Several far-sighted ideas and inspirations ensuring the state's livability have sprouted here in the capitol's legislative chambers. The world's largest granite quarries are located in this region's largest and most busy city of Barre. And Vermonters are especially proud of their town of Springfield, long known as the "cradle of inventors."

The cause of many of Vermont's 400-plus lakes and ponds is due to a great sheet of ice that once covered the state. Most of the Piedmont's bodies of water were formed by massive glaciers scouring out low spots in the rocky earth. Thus it is the ancient Ice Age that Vermonters and visitors can be thankful for. It was this great phenomenon in the earth's history that created the state's gorgeous lake country. Unending recreational opportunities await eager guests.

Lake Memphremagog, meaning in Indian "beautiful waters," is the second-largest lake in the state. Owned jointly by Vermont and Quebec, this beloved lake is easily accessible via the John F. Kennedy Memorial Highway, Interstate 91. Lake Memphremagog's port city, Newport, known locally as the Border City, is a quaint, little city serving as a popular gateway between Canada and New England. The cleanliness and beautiful mountain setting of this vacation resort beckons many a summer traveler to stop and admire its charm. Each spring scores of anglers crowd the railway platform adjoining Lake 'Magog, playfully competing for the first strike of the day. In nearby Newport Center the exciting Troy Falls provides more examples of Vermont's natural endowments.

Picturesque Lake Willoughby, located to the southeast, near Westmore, has been proclaimed the nation's most beautiful body of water. This U-shaped lake is surrounded by a peaceful, rural farming community, which enhances the lake's reputation as a wilderness beauty. It has been compared to Lake Lucerne of Switzerland. Because the residents live on farms back in the hilly country, a local expression explains that the community of Westmore is known by its recreational name of Willoughby Lake in the summer, but in the winter it is called by its given name.

By hopping around May Pond and Crystal Lake via Route 16, the meandering traveler will discover Glover, another peaceful, little village with a not-so-peaceful history. In 1810 a group of well-intentioned local men went to work changing the course of Long Pond to provide mill power. After a few hours of digging the new channel, the entire north shore suddenly began to wash away. Cascading waters rushed north covering barns, mills, and trees on its way to Lake Memphremagog. The pond was drained in 90 minutes. In good humor the lake was later renamed "Runaway Pond."

Other important and scenic waterways in the Piedmont and Northeast Highlands regions include the Connecticut and Winooski rivers and Lake Averill. The Connecticut forms the entire eastern border. In the violent days of raiding and counter-raiding by the white man and Indians, this long river was a busy route for canoes. The beautiful Winooski River canyon, often compared with the grandeur of western river canyons, cuts a deep 4,000-foot valley through the main range of the Green Mountains. The remote Averill ponds are reportedly excellent sites for fishing and hunting. Located in Vermont's northeastern frontier, the two ponds—Great Averill Pond, and the adjoining Little Averill Pond—are typical of Essex County's remote lakes and ponds. Several are generously stocked with fingerlings dropped from low-flying aircraft by the Vermont Fish and Game Department. Many of these peaceful fishing havens are reachable by hiking trails only.

At nearby Beecher Falls, the Ethan Allen furniture factory offers guided tours. Here skilled Vermont craftsmen construct this famous colonial-style furniture.

Heading south out of the northeast wilderness area, the touring sightseer is certain to be entertained by pleasant St. Johnsbury, the largest city in Vermont's northeastern sector. Home of the Fairbanks-Morse Scales and Cary Maple Sugar, St. Johnsbury has a refreshing cosmopolitan flavor. A significant cultural achievement, this busy little community maintains three fascinating museums: the Fairbanks

Museum of Natural Science and Planetarium; the Maple Grove Maple Museum; and a unique art gallery and library at the St. Johnsbury Athenaeum. An alert sightseer can view one of the country's finest collections of mammals, birds, and fossils at the Fairbanks Museum; witness sap boiling at the world's largest maple sugar candy factory at the Maple Grove Museum; and study a first-rate collection of art at the nearby Athenaeum.

A short jaunt west of St. Johnsbury on State Highway 2 is Cabot, home of New England's largest and most modern manufacturer of cheddar cheese and butter. Excellent buys on cheddar cheese, and a demonstration of the interesting cheddaring process, allows the visitor another fun holiday stop.

Guests and residents alike often take time to discover, and rediscover, the secrets of Vermont's state capital, Montpelier, and the busy, industrious work of neighboring Barre.

From afar guests to Montpelier will spy the gold dome of the majestic Capitol Building. From the top of the shimmering dome, the Roman goddess of agriculture, Ceres, watches over her people with a gentle, motherly smile. Vermonters' deep concern for environmental controls are put into law in these legislative chambers. The independent character of Vermont and its people is reflected by the progressive laws that are passed here. Vermonters, always a people ready to fight to protect what is rightfully theirs, have been leaders in the field of environmental control ever since they insisted on controlling billboard advertising. In 1973 the state legislature enacted the beverage container deposit law, and is also a leader in pollution abatement laws. An added distinction, which further documents Vermonters' farsightedness, is the little known fact that this state was the very first to provide for absentee voting.

In neighboring Barre, the Rock of Ages Company operates the world's largest granite quarries and the world's largest granite finishing plant. Comparable to its sister city Proctor, and its marble industry, Barre has no serious competitor for its granite.

The southern counties of the Piedmont—Orange, Windsor, and Windham—are dotted with several points of interest for the Vermont newcomer. Located on Interstate Highway 89 and 91 are the towns of Sharon, Norwich, Windsor, Bellows Falls, Putney, and Brattleboro. Each tells a new and interesting story.

Sharon is the birthplace of Joseph Smith, founder of the Mormon Church. Dedicated to Smith's religious inspiration is a giant 39-ton granite monolith, said to be the world's largest. Each of the 38½ vertical feet of the monolith represents one year of the prophet's life.

Passing through industrial Hartford and White River Junction, the visitor will want to keep an eye out for Norwich. Located in the northeast corner of Windsor County, this charming village typifies a scene of Old New England. A Paul Revere bell hangs in the steeple of the handsome and very old First Congregational Church.

Motoring south along Interstate 91, the sign ''Welcome to Windsor'' will greet the Vermont traveler. Here, in 1777, in a local tavern, gathered 72 chosen delegates to sign the first Constitution dedicating the ''free and independent State of Vermont.'' The tavern is known today as the Old Constitution House. The historic building is preserved and open to the public.

Continuing south along U.S. Highway 91, Bellows Falls is sure to attract railroad buffs. A vast collection of every conceivable type of caboose, steam locomotive, luxurious passenger car, and freight car is on display here. ''Steamtown, U.S.A.'' is Bellows Falls' more familiar name. Saxtons River, the Piedmont's southernmost border, flows into ''Steamtown.''

Immediately south is Putney, home of ''Santa's Land, U.S.A.,'' a child's fantasy come true. And farther south along Interstate Highway 91 is historic Brattleboro, where ''no farmer tended his fields without an ample supply of powder and ball.'' Indian raids were a normal part of everyday living here, in the early settlers' days. Today Brattleboro is the home of the dairy industry's national headquarters, the Holstein-Frisian Association.

Off the beaten paths in the Piedmont region are four very interesting towns well worth the travel time. These are Plymouth, Quechee, Tunbridge, and Groton.

Plymouth, birthplace of ''Silent Cal'' Coolidge, is a favorite stop. It was here in his father's home that the 30th President was sworn into the highest office. When news of President Warren G. Harding's death reached then-Vice President Coolidge, ''Silent Cal'' was sworn into the presidency by his father at night by the light of a kerosene lamp. Those unique and dramatic surroundings have captured the romantic imaginations of the American people ever since the event.

The ''Tunbridge Little World's Fair'' is an annual event enjoyed by many. Held every autumn, the country fair has been a local tradition for over 100 years. Located off of Interstate Highway 89, this rustic little community anchors the southern part of Orange County. Five covered bridges are the pride of the Tunbridge natives.

At a midway point, Groton is the home of five state parks in one, where the outdoors enthusiast can relax with a fishing pole, swim in one of seven ponds, or take a hike in the area's many acres of beautiful open space. This peaceful community is accessible via State Highway 302.

Vermont's Piedmont and Northeast Highlands are a playground come true, and these eastern regions of beautiful Vermont are sure to delight everyone.

Beautiful America Publishing Company

The nation's foremost publisher of quality color photography

Current Books

Alaska
Arizona
Boston
British Columbia
California
California Vol. II
California Coast
California Desert
California Missions
California Mountains
Chicago
Colorado
Dallas
Delaware
Denver
Florida
Georgia
Hawaii
Idaho
Illinois
Indiana
Kentucky
Las Vegas
Los Angeles, 200 Years

Maryland
Massachusetts
Michigan
Michigan Vol. II
Minnesota
Missouri
Montana
Montana Vol. II
Monterey Peninsula
Mormon
Mt. Hood (Oregon)
Nevada
New Jersey
New Mexico
New York
New York City
Northern California
Northern California Vol. II
North Carolina
North Idaho
Ohio
Oklahoma
Orange County
Oregon

Oregon Vol. II
Oregon Coast
Oregon Country
Pacific Coast
Pennsylvania
Pittsburgh
San Diego
San Francisco
San Juan Islands
Seattle
Tennessee
Texas
Utah
Utah Country
Vancouver U.S.A.
Vermont
Virginia
Volcano Mt. St. Helens
Washington
Washington Vol. II
Washington, D.C.
Wisconsin
Wyoming
Yosemite National Park

Forthcoming Books

Alabama
Arkansas
Baltimore
Connecticut
Detroit
The Great Lakes
Houston
Kansas

Kauai
Maine
Maui
Mississippi
New England
New Hampshire
North Dakota

Oahu
Phoenix
Rhode Island
Rocky Mountains
South Carolina
South Dakota
West Virginia

Large Format, Hardbound Books

Beautiful America
Beauty of California
Beauty of Oregon

Beauty of Washington
Glory of Nature's Form
Volcanoes of the West

Lewis & Clark Country
Western Impressions